WINTER OLYMPIC

S0-BYL-216

BOBSLEIGH, LUGE, AND SKELETON

by Robin Johnson

Words that are defined in the glossary are in **bold** type the first time they appear in the text.

A table of abbreviations used for the names of countries appears on page 32.

Crabtree editor: Adrianna Morganelli
Proofreader: Crystal Sikkens
Editorial director: Kathy Middleton
Production coordinator and prepress technician: Katherine Berti
Developed for Crabtree Publishing Company by RJF Publishing LLC (www.RJFpublishing.com)
Editor: Jacqueline Laks Gorman
Designer: Tammy West, Westgraphix LLC
Photo Researcher: Edward A. Thomas
Indexer: Nila Glikin

Photo Credits:
Associated Press: Wide World Photos: p. 24
Corbis: Mirko Guarriello/epa: p. 6; Wally McNamee: p. 10; Erich Schlegel/Dallas Morning News: p. 22; Chris Trotman/Duomo: p. 27
Getty Images: p. 4, 9; AFP: front cover, p. 8, 11, 16, 18, 20, 25, 26; Bongarts: p. 2, 12, 14, 15, 19
Jennifer Wenzel/Icon SMI: p. 28
Laszlo Balogh/Reuters/Landov: p. 17
Wikipedia: Uncleweed: p. 29

Cover: Canada's Pierre Lueders (front) and Lascelles Brown begin a bobsleigh run at the 2006 Winter Olympics.

CONTENTS

Sliding Events 2
On the Right Track 4
Bobsleigh 6
Four-Man Bobsleigh 8
Two-Man Bobsleigh 10
Two-Woman Bobsleigh 12
Luge 14
Men's Singles Luge 16
Women's Singles Luge 18
Doubles Luge 20
Skeleton 22
Men's Skeleton 24
Women's Skeleton 26
A Snapshot of the Vancouver 2010 Winter Olympics 28
Glossary 30
Find Out More 31
Index 32

Library and Archives Canada Cataloguing in Publication

Johnson, Robin (Robin R.)
     Bobsleigh, luge, and skeleton / Robin Johnson.
(Winter Olympic sports)
Includes index.
ISBN 978-0-7787-4024-7 (bound).--ISBN 978-0-7787-4043-8 (pbk.).

     1. Bobsledding--Juvenile literature. 2. Tobogganing--Juvenile literature. 3. Coasting (Winter sports)--Juvenile literature. 4. Winter Olympics--Juvenile literature. I. Title. II. Series: Winter Olympic sports

GV856.J64 2009   j796.9'5   C2009-903221-X

Library of Congress Cataloging-in-Publication Data

Johnson, Robin (Robin R.)
     Bobsleigh, luge, and skeleton / Robin Johnson.
        p. cm. -- (Winter Olympic sports)
     Includes index.
     ISBN 978-0-7787-4043-8 (pbk. : alk. paper)
   -- ISBN 978-0-7787-4024-7 (reinforced library binding : alk. paper)
     1. Bobsledding. 2. Coasting (Winter sports) 3. Winter sports.
I. Title.

GV856.J64 2010
796.9'5--dc22
                                   2009029496

Crabtree Publishing Company

www.crabtreebooks.com   1-800-387-7650
Copyright © 2010 CRABTREE PUBLISHING COMPANY. All rights reserved. No part of this publication may be reproduced, stored in a retrieval system or be transmitted in any form or by any means, electronic, mechanical, photocopying, recording, or otherwise, without the prior written permission of Crabtree Publishing Company. In Canada: We acknowledge the financial support of the Government of Canada through the Book Publishing Industry Development Program (BPIDP) for our publishing activities.

Published in Canada
Crabtree Publishing
616 Welland Ave.
St. Catharines, ON
L2M 5V6

Published in the United States
Crabtree Publishing
PMB16A
350 Fifth Ave., Suite 3308
New York, NY 10118

Published in the United Kingdom
Crabtree Publishing
White Cross Mills
High Town, Lancaster
LA1 4XS

Published in Australia
Crabtree Publishing
386 Mt. Alexander Rd.
Ascot Vale (Melbourne)
VIC 3032

SLIDING EVENTS

Bobsleigh, luge, and skeleton are high-tech sled races that take place on steep, curving tracks at extremely high speeds.

Brazil's four-man bobsleigh team at the start of a run.

SLIDING THROUGH HISTORY

People have been using wooden sleds to travel on snow and ice for centuries. In the 1870s, British guests at a **resort** in Switzerland crafted the first steerable sleds. Today, Olympic bobsleigh, luge, and skeleton competitors speed down refrigerated tracks on **aerodynamic** racing machines.

LET IT SLIDE

Sliding sports are some of the fastest events at the Winter Olympic Games. Sleds—which are powered only by racers and the force of gravity—reach incredible speeds of more than 84 MPH (135 km/h)!

NEED FOR SPEED

Competitors in all three sliding sports race against the clock in a series of **heats**. The times are added together, and the lowest combined time wins. Bobsleigh and skeleton are timed to the hundredth of a second. Luge is timed to the thousandth of a second.

OLYMPICS FACT FILE

- The Olympic Games were first held in Olympia, in ancient Greece, around 3,000 years ago. They took place every four years until they were abolished in 393 A.D. A Frenchman named Pierre Coubertin (1863–1937) revived the Games, and the first modern Olympics—which featured only summer sports—were held in Athens in 1896.

- The first Olympic Winter Games were held in 1924 in Chamonix, France. The Winter Games were then held every four years except in 1940 and 1944 (because of World War II), taking place in the same year as the Summer Games, until 1992.

- The International Olympic Committee decided to stage the Summer and Winter Games in different years, so there was only a two-year gap before the next Winter Games were held in 1994. They have been held every four years from that time.

- The symbol of the Olympic Games is five interlocking colored rings. Together, they represent the union of the five regions of the world— Africa, the Americas, Asia, Europe, and Oceania (Australia and the Pacific Islands)—as athletes come together to compete in the Games.

Julia Anashkina (RUS)
slides down the luge track.

ON THE RIGHT TRACK

Olympic bobsleigh, luge, and skeleton events all run on the same track. Each sliding track in the world is unique, but built and maintained to exact **specifications**.

WHISTLE WHILE YOU SLIDE

Sliding events at the Vancouver 2010 Olympics will be held at the Whistler Sliding Centre. The 0.9-mile (1.45-km) track has 16 curves and the highest vertical drop of any track in the world.

THE GREAT INTERNATIONAL SLED RACE

On February 12, 1883, the first international sliding contest took place in Switzerland. Competitors from seven countries raced down a 2.5-mile (4-km) track connecting two villages. A Swiss mailman and an Australian student tied for the win, completing the course in just over nine minutes.

ICE AGE

The first sliding track was built in St. Moritz, Switzerland, in 1903. It was used in the 1928 and 1948 Winter Olympics, and is the only natural-ice track still used in international competitions. Today, sliding tracks are made of concrete, covered by a thick layer of **artificial** ice.

G WHIZ!

Racers on sliding tracks experience powerful **G-force**. G-force is the pull of gravity (G) that keeps athletes and their sleds from flying off winding tracks. Track G-force often reaches 5 G, or five times the normal pull of gravity!

DID YOU KNOW?

- There are only 16 sliding tracks used for international races in the world.

- Olympic tracks must include straight sections, curves, and combinations of curves.

- Curves on sliding tracks are often given names. Some of the curves at Whistler are called "Thunderbird," "Shiver," and "Lynx."

BANK ON IT

High banked walls help keep competitors on track as they speed around dangerous curves. Racers who lose control of their sleds and veer off track run the risk of serious injuries — or even death.

LEARN THE LINGO

Bank — the sloped wall of a sliding track
Kreisel — a loop on a sliding track that forms a circle
Labyrinth — a stretch of track that has right and left curves, but no straight sections
Lip — a barrier at the top of a track that keeps racers from sliding off
Vertical drop — the change in height from the top to the bottom of a track

BOBSLEIGH

In bobsleigh races, teams of two or four people work together to push their sleds from standing starts and ride them through a series of turns at extreme speeds.

The championship team of Sandra Kiriasis and Anja Schneiderheinze (GER) begin a run in the two-woman bobsleigh.

BOBSLEIGH 101

A bobsleigh team begins by running with the sled for about 165 feet (50 m), pushing it as fast as possible to gain **momentum**. Then the crew jumps in and races down the track at speeds of more than 84 MPH (135 km/h).

SUPER STATS

At the 2006 Olympics, the winning two-man bobsleigh team of Kevin Kuske and André Lang (GER) spent a total of 3:43.38 on the course. The times of their four runs were 55.28 seconds, 55.73 seconds, 56.01 seconds, and 56.36 seconds—less than one minute per run!

DID YOU KNOW?

• A typical bobsleigh race lasts about 55 to 60 seconds.

• Bobsleigh got its name because early racers bobbed back and forth to pick up speed on the tracks. (It didn't work.)

THE CREW

Every bobsleigh team has a **driver** and a **brakeman**. The driver jumps into the sled first and steers it carefully down the track. The brakeman—who is usually the fastest crew member—jumps into the sled last and stops it at the end of the race. Four-man bobsleigh teams also have two **pushers**.

THE SLED

A bobsleigh is made of **fiberglass** and steel, with four smooth steel runners. Ropes attached to the two front runners allow the driver to steer, while brake handles allow the brakeman to slow and stop the sled.

DRESS FOR SUCCESS

Bobsledders wear skintight racing suits made of a stretchy material, shoes with small spikes on them, and helmets. Drivers also must wear protective goggles.

OFF TO A GOOD START

The start—which takes about five seconds—is the most important part of the race. Mistakes made at the beginning of a run affect the speed of the sled throughout the race.

UNDER A MINUTE

The four-man bobsleigh team from East Germany that won the gold medal at the 1980 Winter Olympics did something no other team had ever done—they broke the one-minute barrier for a single run. On their first run, they recorded a time of 59.86 seconds. The next day, on their third run, they bettered that time with 59.73 seconds!

IF AT FIRST ...

Brian Shimer (USA) refused to give up! He participated in bobsleigh in 1988, 1992, 1994, and 1998 and failed to medal every time. He came back in 2002 at the age of 39 with a four-man team. After the first two races, they were only in fifth place. Then, on the fourth and last race, they turned in the fastest time of the competition and pulled into third place. Shimer finally had his medal—a bronze.

LEARN THE LINGO

Loading—entering a sled after a running start

Push—the start of a bobsleigh race

FOUR-MAN BOBSLEIGH

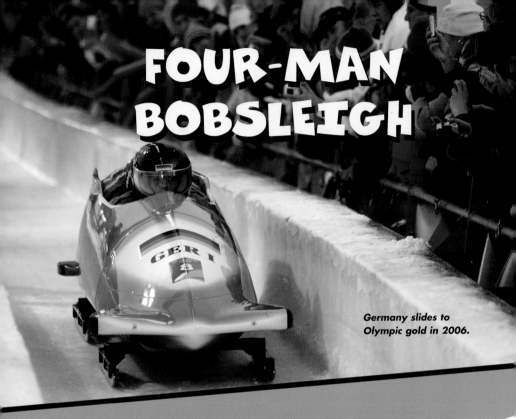

Germany slides to Olympic gold in 2006.

The four-man bobsleigh was the only sliding race featured at the first Winter Games. It **debuted** in 1924 and has been included in almost every Olympics since then.

RACE BASICS

The four-man bobsleigh is run in four heats held over two days. The team with the lowest combined time wins.

MIDDLE MEN

The pushers are usually the strongest members of the four-man crew. They help get the heavy bobsleigh moving quickly at the start of a race. Then they jump into the middle spots and—without moving a muscle—enjoy the ride.

EXCEPTIONAL EDDIE EAGAN

Eddie Eagan (USA) is the only athlete to win gold medals at both the Summer and Winter Olympics. He was the light heavyweight boxing champ at the 1920 Summer Games and a member of the victorious U.S. four-man bobsleigh team at the 1932 Winter Games.

2006 OLYMPIC MEDALISTS: GOLD: GERMANY

BRINGING THE HEAT

The Jamaican bobsleigh team coolly slid into the Winter Games for the first time in 1988. The inexperienced team—who came from a tropical island with no snow—were not able to complete the competition. After a spectacular crash on their third run, the team walked with their sled across the finish line!

CALLING ALL BOBSLEDDERS!

Three of the members of the 1928 U.S. bobsleigh team were picked after they answered a newspaper ad, even though they had never seen a bobsleigh before! The team was steered to a gold-medal finish by driver Billy Fiske, who was just 16 years old.

The Jamaicans in action in 1988.

TWO-MAN BOBSLEIGH

The two-man bobsleigh race has been a Winter Olympic event since 1932. Run in four heats over two days, the event tests a pair's strength, speed, and steering skills.

A celebration by the medal winners in the two-man bobsleigh event at the 1992 Olympics.

2006 OLYMPIC MEDALISTS: GOLD: KEVIN KUSKE & ANDRÉ LANG (GER)

The United States captured gold at the 1932 and 1936 Games. Since then, Germany and Switzerland have dominated the bobsleigh competition.

MISSING MEDAL

No silver medal was awarded in the two-man bobsleigh at the 1998 Olympics. Canada and Italy tied for first place and shared the gold.

A LUCKY BRAKE

German bobsledder Christoph Langen's brakeman was injured just two weeks before the 2002 Olympics. Langen partnered with a last-minute replacement and won the event in the final heat.

Canada's Pierre Lueders (front) and Lascelles Brown were the silver medal winners in 2006.

COOL RUNNERS

It is illegal for bobsleigh teams in all events to heat the runners on their sleds. Hot runners melt the ice on the track and increase a sled's speed. The temperature of the runners is checked before each race.

DEAD HEAT

At the 1968 Games, Italy and West Germany tied for first place in the two-man event, each recording a total time of 4:41.54. Italy's Eugenio Monti and Luciano de Paolis were awarded the gold medal for having scored the fastest time in one of the heats.

REPEAT PERFORMANCE

Gustav Weder and Donat Acklin (SUI) are the first bobsledders to achieve back-to-back gold medals in the two-man event. They won at the 1992 Olympics, and then, two years later, edged out their fellow Swiss team— which included Acklin's younger brother—to capture gold again.

TWO-WOMAN BOBSLEIGH

The two-woman bobsleigh event has only been on the Olympic program since 2002, but the race is quickly gaining momentum.

A victorious run for Vonetta Flowers (top) and Jill Bakken of the United States in 2002.

RACE BASICS

The women's bobsleigh race has the same rules and requirements as the men's event. The race is run in four heats held over two days.

2006 OLYMPIC MEDALISTS: GOLD: SANDRA KIRIASIS & ANJA SCHNEIDERHEINZE (GER)

SUPER STATS

The women's bobsleigh race has been contested at only two Olympic Games. Germany has won the most medals so far, with one of each color. The United States is close behind with one gold and one silver, while Italy has a single bronze in the event.

WEIGH TO GO!

Bobsleigh teams in all events are weighed with their sleds at the finish line. Since heavier sleds slide downhill faster than lighter sleds, there are strict weight limits for each event. Lighter teams can attach weights to their sleds before the race begins, but teams that exceed the weight limits are **disqualified** from the race.

BOB AND LUGE

Gerda Weissensteiner (ITA) and Susi Erdmann (GER) are the only athletes to win Olympic medals in both bobsleigh and luge events. Both women scored in luge races before sliding over to the bobsleigh scene.

SOCCER STAR

Shauna Rohbock (USA), who won silver in the two-woman bobsleigh in 2006, played professional soccer for the San Diego Star of the Women's United Soccer Association in 2003.

SWEET SMELL OF SUCCESS

When brakewoman Vonetta Flowers (USA) won the women's bobsleigh in 2002, she became the first black athlete to earn gold at the Winter Olympic Games. Flowers took up bobsleigh after she failed to make the U.S. Olympic track and field team.

WHO'S COUNTING?

Only seconds separated the top three teams in the two-woman bobsleigh event at the 2006 Winter Olympics. The first-place Germans had a time of 3:49.98, the second-place Americans had a time of 3:50.69, and the third-place Italians had a time of 3:51.01.

MULTIPLE ENTRIES

In Olympic bobsleigh competition, each nation may enter up to three sleds in each event (the two-man, four-man, and two-woman contests).

MOVING UP

Sandra Kiriasis (GER) won a silver medal in the two-woman's bobsleigh event at the 2002 Winter Olympics while competing under the name of Sandra Prokoff. She got married in 2004 and changed her name. She also changed bobsleigh partners and came back to the Games in 2006, this time winning gold.

pod

Kufen (runner)

steel

Anna Orlova (LAT) competes in women's singles luge.

LUGE

Luge sliders compete in men's singles, women's singles, or doubles races. All three events have been contested at the Winter Olympics since 1964.

LUGE 101

Luge competitors lie on their backs and race feet-first down tracks on open sleds. Racers steer by applying pressure to the sleds' runners—which are sensitive to even the slightest touch—with their legs and shoulders. To slow down or stop, racers drag their feet on the ice and pull up on the runners. There are no brakes on the sleds.

LEARN THE LINGO

Kufens—the runners on a luge
Luge—a sled and the sliding race in which it is used
Pod—the seat on a luge
Slider—a luge racer (sometimes called a luger)

SECONDS TO SPARE

To win the 2006 gold medal in the luge, Armin Zoeggeler (ITA) put up runs of 51.718 seconds, 51.414 seconds, 51.430 seconds, and 51.526 seconds, for a total time of 3:26.088. The second-place finisher had a total time of 3:26.198, while the third-place finisher had a time of 3:26.445.

THE SLED

A luge is an open fiberglass sled with a seat and two runners. Blades called steels are attached to the runners and are the only parts of the sled that touch the track. Steels are the most important part of a luge and are adjusted and polished often to improve performance.

DRESS FOR SUCCESS

Sliders wear helmets with face shields; skintight racing suits; gloves with small, sharp spikes; and smooth-soled, aerodynamic shoes called booties.

FIRST MEDAL WINNERS

When the first Olympic men's singles luge event was held in 1964, the gold medal went to Thomas Köhler (GDR). In the first Olympic women's luge event, held the same year, Ortun Enderlein (GDR) emerged with the gold medal.

THEY'VE GOT RHYTHM

Luge sliders often have backgrounds in skateboarding, snowboard, and gynmnastics. These sports all require a good sense of rhythm and an ability to react to different movements and sensations, just like luge.

Albert Demtschenko (RUS) at the end of his silver medal winning run.

MEN'S SINGLES LUGE

Georg Hackl (GER), one of the best lugers in history, in action in 2006.

The men's singles luge event tests a slider's ability to handle intense pressure—and G-forces—without losing his head.

WHAT A LUGER!

Legendary slider Georg Hackl (GER) is the only luge racer to slide his way to the **podium** in five consecutive Games. Hackl took home three golds and two silvers in men's singles competitions from 1988 through 2002.

RACE BASICS

The men's singles luge event is run in four heats over two days. The four-run format is seen only in the Olympics—at most competitions, only two runs are done. The racer with the lowest total time slides away with the top prize.

2006 OLYMPIC MEDALISTS: GOLD: ARMIN ZOEGGELER (ITA)

GOING SOLO

A singles slider begins a race seated on his luge. He pulls on start handles on the track to get the sled moving, then pushes himself along the ice with his hands. Once the luge has picked up speed, the slider lies flat on his back and races down the icy track.

DON'T LOSE IT!

A luger may lose his goggles or the visor attached to his helmet during a run. If he loses anything else, though, he will be disqualified from the competition.

HUNGRY FOR GOLD

Armin Zoeggeler (ITA) has earned the nickname "the cannibal" for eating up the track—and the competition—at his races. He medaled in four consecutive Games, winning gold in the men's singles event in 2002 and 2006.

Armin Zoeggeler (ITA) tests his medal.

LEARN THE LINGO

Crank—using firm pressure to steer a luge
Lose your head—when sliders cannot keep their heads up through high G-force turns
Paddle—pushing on the ice to move forward at the start of a luge race

DISQUALIFIED!

Competitors in all sliding events who push, paddle, or carry their sleds across the finish line—or who cross the finish line without their sleds—are disqualified from the race.

WOMEN'S SINGLES LUGE

Sylke Otto (GER) enjoys her victory in the women's singles luge in 2006.

In the women's singles event, even the slightest movement can mean the difference between winning and losing.

2006 OLYMPIC MEDALISTS: GOLD: SYLKE OTTO (GER)

Silke Kraushaar (GER) concentrates while taking a slide on the course.

DID YOU KNOW?

- German sliders have dominated both women's and men's Olympic luge, winning a total of 65 medals — including 25 golds — over 12 Games.

- Silke Kraushaar (GER) slid to gold in the 1998 women's singles luge, edging out the silver medal winner by only two-thousandths of a second!

- At the 2002 and 2006 Olympics, Germany **swept** the women's singles event, winning every medal that was awarded.

RACE BASICS

The women's singles luge event is run in four heats over two days. Women use the same track as men, but they start the race farther down the course.

GOLDEN GIRLS

Steffi Walter (GER) and Sylke Otto (GER) are the only sliders to win the women's singles event twice. Walter won in 1984 and 1988, and Otto won in 2002 and 2006.

SCANDAL!

At the 1968 Games, three members of the East German women's team were disqualified for illegally heating the runners on their sleds. The women — who had placed first, second, and fourth — were disqualified.

GRANDMA LUGE

Anne Abernathy (ISV) is the oldest woman ever to compete in the Olympic Winter Games. Affectionately nicknamed "Grandma Luge," she raced in the women's singles event in 2002 at the age of 48. She qualified in 2006 but suffered an injury and could not compete.

BACK ON TRACK

At the 1964 Games in Innsbruck, Austria, a shortage of snow threatened to cancel the first Olympic luge competition. The Austrian army saved the day by carving out and carrying 20,000 bricks of ice from a mountaintop to repair the track!

DOUBLES LUGE

Andreas and Wolfgang Linger (AUT) slide to victory.

Doubles luge events test a pair's ability to work together while lying down on the job!

RACE BASICS

The doubles luge event is made up of two heats run on a single day. Doubles races begin at the same spot on the track as women's singles races.

2006 OLYMPIC MEDALISTS: GOLD: ANDREAS LINGER & WOLFGANG LINGER (AUT)

ON THE DOUBLE

In the doubles event, sliders begin the race seated on their sled with their legs stretched out in front of them. The front racer—who is strapped to the sled—pulls on the track handles to rock the sled back and forth and propel it out of the starting gate. Meanwhile, the back racer holds onto the straps. Both racers then use their hands to push the sled forward quickly down the track. Once the sled is up to speed, both competitors lie on their backs (the front racer on top of the back racer) and speed together through the winding course.

MIX IT UP

The doubles luge race is technically a **mixed** event, which means that teams made up of both men and women can compete. No women have ever raced in doubles luge at the Olympic Games, however.

BROTHERLY LOVE

Andreas and Wolfgang Linger (AUT), who won the gold medal in doubles luge in 2006, are brothers. They have competed in luge since 1992 and joined the Austrian national team in 2000.

FAST FRIENDS

Stefan Krausse and Jan Behrendt (GER) are the only doubles sliders to win medals in four Olympic Games. The pair—who have been friends since they were six years old—slid to the podium together from 1988 through 1998.

CUTTING IT CLOSE

The gold medal winners in the 2006 doubles luge posted a total time of 1:34.497 for their two runs of 47.028 seconds and 47.469 seconds. The silver medal winners had a total time of 1:34.809, while the bronze medal winners had a total time of 1:34.930.

FIRST MEDALS

The first Olympic medals ever awarded in doubles luge, in 1964, went to Josef Feistmantl and Manfred Stengl (AUT), who posted a time of 1:41.62.

SILVER: ANDRÉ FLORSCHÜTZ & TORSTEN WUSTLICH (GER)
BRONZE: : GERHARD PLANKENSTEINER & OSWALD HASELRIEDER (ITA)

SKELETON

Skeleton is an individual sport in which daring racers speed head-first down bone-chilling tracks.

Eric Bernotas (USA) jumps on his sled to begin his run.

In the men's skeleton at the 2006 Olympics, gold medal winner Duff Gibson (CAN) beat his countryman, Jeff Pain, by only 0.26 seconds! Gibson's total time was 1:55.88, while Pain—who almost lost control of his sled on one of the last turns—put up a total time of 1:56.14.

OLYMPIC HISTORY

Men's skeleton races were held at the 1928 and 1948 Winter Games. The sport returned to the Olympics in 2002, with both men's and women's events included on the program.

SKELETON 101

Competitors begin skeleton races by **sprinting** with their sleds for about 165 feet (50 m). Then they dive onto the sleds and speed on their stomachs down the tracks. Racers steer by applying slight pressure to the sleds with their shoulders and knees and by shifting their body weight. They stop by gradually **decelerating** at the end of a race.

GEAR UP

Like competitors in other sliding events, skeleton riders wear stretchy, skintight racing suits. They wear spiked shoes that grip the ice at the running start of the race. They must also wear helmets with chin guards.

WHAT'S IN A NAME

- Skeleton is the name of both the sled and the race in which it is used.
- Skeleton got its name because the first sleds used in the sport had bony metal frames that looked like human skeletons!
- The sport of skeleton was called "tobogganing" in early competitions.

THE SLED

Skeletons are low, heavy sleds made of fiberglass and steel. They have one pod, two polished runners, two handles—and no brakes!

OLYMPIC MEDALS

The United States has won the most medals overall in the Olympics in skeleton.

Rank	Country	Gold	Silver	Bronze	Total Medals
1	United States	3	3	0	6
2	Canada	1	1	1	3
3	Switzerland	1	0	2	3
4	Italy	1	0	0	1
5	Great Britain	0	1	3	4
6	Austria	0	1	0	1

MEN'S SKELETON

Make no bones about it: men's skeleton is a fast-flying, head-first display of talent and athleticism.

Gold medal winner Duff Gibson (CAN) navigates a run.

When skeleton was first contested at the 1928 Olympics, each racer took three runs down the track. Twenty years later, the number of runs doubled to six. At the 2002 and 2006 Games, only two runs were done. In 2010, each skeleton racer will have four runs.

RACE BASICS

The men's skeleton event is run in four heats over a period of two days. The two-day format tests a racer's ability to cope with the intense pressures of Olympic competition. The times are added together, and the lowest time wins.

SIBLING RIVALRY

The first gold medal in men's skeleton was awarded to Jennison Heaton (USA) in 1928. He beat the silver medalist—his younger brother John—by one second. John came back 20 years later and won another silver.

DID YOU KNOW?

• *Duff Gibson (CAN) is the oldest athlete to win gold in an individual event at the Winter Games. In 2006, he slid to victory in the men's skeleton race at the age of 39.*

• *A turn on the 2006 Olympic sliding track is named in honor of legendary slider Nino Bibbia (ITA). Bibbia competed in both skeleton and bobsleigh at the 1948 Games, taking home gold in the skeleton.*

HOORAY FOR SHEA

Skeleton racer Jim Shea (USA) competed at the 2002 Olympic Games with a photograph of his grandfather, Jack, tucked inside his helmet. Jack—who won two gold medals in speed skating at the 1932 Games—was killed in a car accident shortly before his grandson's race. Jim won the men's skeleton event by five-hundredths of a second.

An emotional Jim Shea (USA) celebrates his victory in the 2002 men's skeleton race.

WOMEN'S SKELETON

Alex Coomber (GBR) during the women's skeleton final in 2002.

In women's skeleton, racers sprint, leap, slide, and steer to find the perfect line to the finish line.

2006 OLYMPIC MEDALISTS: GOLD: MAYA PEDERSEN (SUI)

SUPER STATS

LEARN THE LINGO

Line — the best path for a sled to take on a track

Mind run — when competitors **visualize** their run on a course before a race

Prone — the position skeleton racers take lying face- down on their stomachs

Tristan Gale (USA), in front, enjoys her victory.

GALE FORCE

When Tristan Gale (USA) slid to victory at the 2002 Olympics, it marked two important firsts. It was the first gold medal ever awarded in the women's skeleton event, and it was the first time that she captured a medal in an international race!

RACE BASICS

The women's skeleton event is run in four heats over two days. It has the same rules, starting point, and need for speed as the men's event.

COOL AS A CU-COOMBER

Alexandra "Alex" Coomber (GBR) coolly slid to a bronze-medal finish at the 2002 Games. Remarkably, she did so with a broken wrist! Coomber — who was injured in training just 10 days before the race — concealed the injury from her coaches so she could compete at the Olympics.

ANIMAL OLYMPIANS

Penguins are the super sliders of the animal world! Many of these cool birds lie on their stomachs and slide down snowy hills and icebergs.

A SNAPSHOT OF THE VANCOUVER 2010 WINTER OLYMPICS

BOBSLEIGH, LUGE, AND SKELETON
THE ATHLETES

Everyone is getting ready for Vancouver in 2010! Olympic teams are still being determined. The listings below include the top finishers in a selection of events from the 2009 World Championships for each sport. Who among them will be the athletes to watch in the Vancouver Winter Olympics? Visit the Web site www.vancouver2010.com for more information about the upcoming competitions.

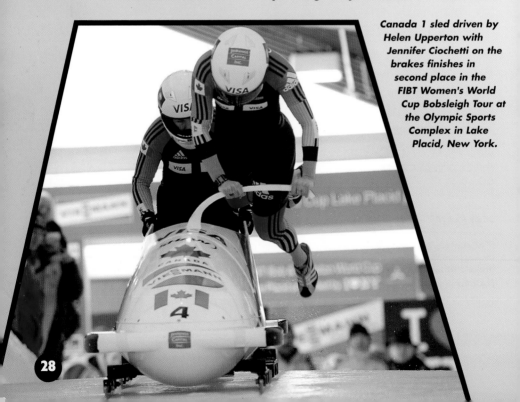

Canada 1 sled driven by Helen Upperton with Jennifer Ciochetti on the brakes finishes in second place in the FIBT Women's World Cup Bobsleigh Tour at the Olympic Sports Complex in Lake Placid, New York.

BOBSLEIGH EVENTS

Two man:
1. Ivo Ruegg,
   Cedric Grand (SUI)
2. Thomas Florschutz,
   Marc Kuhne (GER)
3. Steven Holcomb,
   Curtis Tomasevicz (USA)

Four man:
1. Steven Holcomb,
   Justin Olsen, Steve Mesler,
   Curtis Tomasevicz (USA)
2. Andre Lange, Kevin Kuske,
   Alexander Rodiger,
   Martin Putze (GER)
3. Janis Minins,
   Daumants Dreiskens,
   Oskars Melbardis,
   Intars Dambis (LAT)

Two woman:
1. Nicole Minnichiello,
   Gillian Cooke (GBR)
2. Shauna Rohbock,
   Elana Meyers (USA)
3. Cathleen Martini,
   Janine Tischer (GER)

SKELETON EVENTS

Men — singles:
1. Gregor Stahli (SUI)
2. Adam Pengilly (GBR)
3. Alexander Tretiakov (RUS)

Women — singles:
1. Marion Trott (GER)
2. Amy Williams (GBR)
3. Kerstin Szymkowiak (GER)

Mixed Team:
1. Germany
2. Swirzerland
3. USA

LUGE EVENTS

Men — singles:
1. Felix loch (GER)
2. Armin Zoggeler (ITA)
3. Daniel Pfister (AUT)

Men — doubles:
1. Gerhard Plankensteiner,
   Oswald Haselrieder (ITA)
2. André Florschütz,
   Torsten Wustlich (GER)
3. Mark Grimmette,
   Brian Martin (USA)

Women — singles:
1. Erin Hamlin (USA)
2. Natalie Geisenberger (GER)
3. Natalia Yakushenko (UKR)

Mixed-team relay:
1. Germany
2. Austria
3. Latvia

THE VENUE IN VANCOUVER
THE WHISTLER SLIDING CENTRE

- venue capacity: 12,000
- located on Blackcomb Mountain, British Columbia
- elevation: Men's luge handles: 3080 feet (939 m)
- bottom: 2582 feet (787 m)
- highest vertical drop: 498 feet (152 m)

GLOSSARY

aerodynamic Designed to move without being blocked by the wind

artificial Not natural, made by people

bobsledder A bobsleigh competitor

brakeman The last teammate to enter the bobsleigh at the start of a race

Closing Ceremonies An official celebration held at the end of the Olympics

debut To perform something for the first time

decelerating Slowing down

disqualified To be eliminated from competition for not following the rules

driver The teammate who steers the bobsleigh during a race

fiberglass A strong, lightweight material often used on boats and cars

G-force The pull of gravity felt when quickly speeding up or changing direction

heat One run down a course in a competition

mixed Consisting of both men and women

momentum The ability of an object to keep moving

podium A platform on which the winners of an event stand

pushers The people who sit in the middle of the four-man bobsleigh during a race

resort A vacation place

specifications Detailed requirements or measurements about something that is being built

sprinting Running very fast for a short distance

swept Won all the prizes or events in a competition

visualize To picture something in your head

FIND OUT MORE

BOOKS

Eyewitness Olympics (New York: Dorling Kindersley, 2005)

Judd, Ron C. *The Winter Olympics: An Insider's Guide to the Legends, the Lore, and the Games* (Seattle: Mountaineers Books, 2009)

Macy, Sue. *Freeze Frame: A Photographic History of the Winter Olympics* (Washington, DC: National Geographic Society, 2006)

U.S. Olympic Committee. *A Basic Guide to Bobsledding* (Santa Ana, CA: Griffin Publishing, 2002)

WEBSITES

Bobsleigh Canada Skeleton (BCS)   www.bobsleigh.ca
The official site of the Canadian governing group of bobsleigh and skeleton.

Canadian Luge Association   www.luge.ca
The official site of the Canadian governing group of luge.

**International Bobsleigh and
Tobogganing Federation (FIBT)**   www.fibt.com
The site of the international governing group of bobsleigh and skeleton.

International Luge Federation   www.fil-luge.org
The site of the international governing group of luge.

International Olympic Committee   www.olympic.org
The official site of the International Olympic Committee, with information on all Olympic sports.

United States Luge Association   www.usaluge.org
The official site of the U.S. governing group of luge.

USA Bobsled & Skeleton Federation   www.bobsled.teamusa.org
The official site of the U.S. governing group of bobsleigh and skeleton.

INDEX

Abernathy, Anne 19
Acklin, Donat 11
age of athletes 7, 9, 19, 25
Anashkina, Julia 4
Annen, Martin 11
Bakken, Jill 12
basics of races 6, 7, 8, 12, 14, 16, 17, 19, 20, 21, 23, 25, 27
Behrendt, Jan 21
Bernotas, Eric 22
Bibbia, Nino 25
bobsleigh 2, 3, 4, 6–13, 25
brakeman/brakewoman 7, 11, 13
braking 7, 14, 23
Brazil 2
Brown, Lascelles 11
Canada 11, 23, 24, 25
Coomber, Alex 26, 27
Coubertin, Pierre 3
Demtschenko, Albert 15, 17
design of sleds 7, 15, 23
disqualification 13, 17, 19
doubles luge 14, 20–21
driver 7, 9
Eagan, Eddie 8
Enderlein, Ortun 15
Erdmann, Susi 13
Fleming, Valerie 13
Florschütz, André 21
Flowers, Vonetta 12, 13
four-man bobsleigh 2, 7, 8–9
Gale, Tristan 27
gear of athletes 7, 15, 23
Germany 6, 7, 8, 10, 11, 12, 13, 15, 17, 18, 19, 21
Gibson, Duff 23, 24, 25
gravity 3, 5, 16, 17
Hackl, Georg 16
Haselrieder, Oswald 21
Heaton, Jennison 25
Heaton, John 25

heats 3, 8, 10, 11, 12, 16, 19, 20, 25, 27
Hefti, Beat 11
history of Olympic Games 3, 23
history of sliding sports 3, 5, 7, 23
Hollingsworth, Melissa 27
Hüfner, Tatjana 19
injuries and crashes 5, 9, 11, 19, 27
Isacco, Jennifer 13
Jamaica 9
Kiriasis, Sandra 6, 12, 13
Köhler, Thomas 15
Kraushaar, Silke 19
Krausse, Stefan 21
Kuske, Kevin 7, 10
Lang, André 7, 10
Langen, Christoph 11
Linger, Andreas 20, 21
Linger, Wolfgang 20, 21
Lueders, Pierre 11
luge 2, 3, 4, 13, 14–21
men's singles luge 14, 15, 16–17, 19
men's skeleton 24–25
Orlova, Anna 14
Otto, Sylke 18, 19
Pain, Jeff 23, 25
Pedersen, Maya 28
Plankensteiner, Gerhard 23
push 8, 9, 19, 23
pusher 7, 8
Rohbock, Shauna 13
Rubenis, Martins 17
Rudman, Shelley 27
Russia 9, 15, 17
Schneiderheinze, Anja 6, 12
Shea, Jim 25
Shimer, Brian 7
skeleton 2, 3, 4, 22–27

speeds of racing 3, 6, 7, 11, 15
Stähli, Gregor 25
Switzerland 3, 5, 9, 11, 23
tracks 2, 3, 4–5, 6, 7, 11, 14, 17, 19, 20, 21, 22, 23, 25, 27
two-man bobsleigh 7, 10–11
two-woman bobsleigh 6, 12–13
United States 7, 8, 9, 11, 12, 13, 22, 23, 25, 27
Walter, Steffi 19
Weder, Gustav 11
Weissensteiner, Gerda 13
women's singles luge 14, 15, 18–19, 20
women's skeleton 26–27
Wustlich, Torsten 21
Zoeggeler, Armin 15, 16, 17

COUNTRY ABBREVIATIONS

AUT — Austria

CAN — Canada

GBR — Great Britain

GDR — East Germany (1949–1990)

GER — Germany

ISV — Virgin Islands

ITA — Italy

LAT — Latvia

RUS — Russia

SUI — Switzerland

USA — United States of America

Printed in the U.S.A. — CG